A Note to Parents

Eyewitness Readers is a compelling new program for beginning readers, designed in conjunction with leading literacy experts, including Dr. Linda Gambrell, President of the National Reading Conference and past board member of the International Reading Association.

Eyewitness has become the most trusted name in illustrated books, and this new series combines the highly visual *Eyewitness* approach with engaging, easy-to-read stories. Each *Eyewitness Reader* is guaranteed to capture a child's interest while developing his or her reading skills, general knowledge, and love of reading.

The four levels of *Eyewitness Readers* are aimed at different reading abilities, enabling you to choose the books that are exactly right for your children:

Level 1, for **Preschool to Grade 1**
Level 2, for **Grades 1 to 3**
Level 3, for **Grades 2 and 3**
Level 4, for **Grades 2 to 4**

The "normal" age at which a child begins to read can be anywhere from three to eight years old, so these levels are intended only as a general guideline.

No matter which level you select, you can be sure that you are helping your child learn to read, then read to learn!

A DK PUBLISHING BOOK
www.dk.com

Editor Dawn Sirett
Art Editor Jane Horne

Senior Editor Linda Esposito
Senior Art Editor
Diane Thistlethwaite
US Editor Regina Kahney
Production Melanie Dowland
Picture Researcher Angela Anderson
Jacket Designer Simon Oon
Natural History Consultant
Theresa Greenaway

Reading Consultant
Linda B. Gambrell, Ph.D.

First American Edition, 1999
2 4 6 8 10 9 7 5 3 1
Published in the United States by DK Publishing, Inc.
95 Madison Avenue, New York, New York 10016

Library of Congress Cataloging-in-Publication Data
Wallace, Karen.
Busy buzzy bee / by Karen Wallace. -- 1st American ed.
p. cm. -- (Eyewitness readers)
Summary: Explains the behavior and lives of bees, discussing how
they collect nectar from flowers, care for their eggs and queen bee,
and communicate with each other.
ISBN 0-7894-4759-2 (hc). -- ISBN 0-7894-4758-4 (pb)
1. Honeybee Juvenile literature. 2. Bees Juvenile literature.
[1. Honeybee. 2. Bees.] I. Title. II. Series.
QL568. A6W34 1999
595.79'9 --dc21   99-23160
                                              CIP
                                              AC
Color reproduction by Colourscan, Singapore
Printed and bound in Belgium by Proost

The publisher would like to thank the following for
their kind permission to reproduce their photographs:
Key: t=top, b=bottom, l=left, r=right, c=center
Bruce Coleman Ltd: Hans Reinhard 7, 28–29, Jane Burton 20–21,
John Shaw 10–11, Kim Taylor front cover b, 14–15; **Environmental
Images:** Vanessa Miles 6 tr; **NHPA:** Jean-Louis LeMoigne 8 t,
Stephen Dalton front cover tl, back cover tl, back cover tr, 11 tr,
16 t, 22 t, 23 r, 24–25; **Oxford Scientific Films:** David Thompson
4–5, 5 tr, 17 b, 18 t, 32 tl, 32 crb, Scott Camazine 18–19; **Planet
Earth Pictures:** Lythgoe 6 b, Richard Coomber 26–27; **Science
Photo Library:** Eye of Science 10 tr, 32 clb; ©Jerry Young: 30–31.
Additional photography for DK:
Geoff Brightling, Jane Burton, Geoff Dann,
Frank Greenaway, Stephen Oliver, and Kim Taylor.

EYEWITNESS READERS

Level **1** PRESCHOOL-GRADE 1

Busy Buzzy Bee

Written by Karen Wallace

DK PUBLISHING, INC.

Busy Bee has work to do.
She crawls out of her hive.

hive

She spreads her wings.
Busy Bee is looking for a flower.

zzzzzzzzzzzzzzzzzzz

Busy Bee flies
over a stream.

She flies past an oak tree
and into a field.

The field is full of wild flowers.

Busy Bee lands on a flower.

Each flower holds
sweet drops of nectar.
Bees make nectar
into honey.
Nectar and honey
are food for bees.

Busy Bee laps up the nectar
with her long, narrow tongue.
She will take it back to the hive.

nectar

Each flower holds
grains of pollen.
Flower pollen is
food for bees, too.

pollen

The pollen sticks
to Busy Bee's
furry body.

She brings it to the hive
on her two back legs.

Busy Bee is a worker bee.

Inside the hive,
there are thousands like her.
All worker bees are female.

Busy Bee dances a dance.
She waggles her bottom.
She crawls in circles.
Her dance shows
the other workers
the way to find
the flower nectar.

Inside the hive,
the bees make cells.

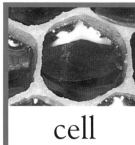

cell

Some are for the honey
the bees make from nectar.

honey cell   pollen cell

Some are for the pollen
the bees have collected.

Some are for the eggs
that the queen bee lays.

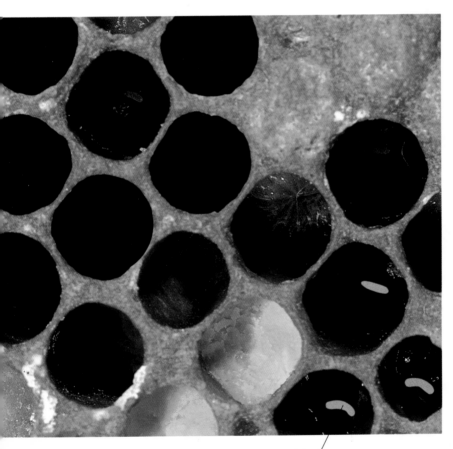

egg cell

Busy Bee has work to do.
First she feeds
the drone bees.

All drones are male.
The drones mate
with a queen bee.

drone

Then Busy Bee
feeds the queen bee.
The queen bee lays
a thousand eggs
every day.

queen
bee

Inside their cells,
the eggs hatch
into bee grubs.

bee grub

Busy Bee and thousands like her take some pollen mixed with honey. They feed it to the hungry grubs.

Busy Bee has work to do.
She feeds the bee grubs
every day.

When the grubs are nine days old
she seals their cells
with waxy covers.

Inside their cells,
the bee grubs change.
They grow legs and wings.
They grow long, narrow tongues.

In twelve days
they change from
grubs to bees.

They crawl out and wait
for their new wings to dry.

Busy Bee and thousands like her
touch the young bees
with their feelers.

feelers

They make them welcome
in the hive.
They feed them honey
from the cells.

Busy Bee has work to do.
The young bees are hungry.
Where can she find
more flower nectar?

Where can
she find more
flower pollen?

27

Look!
Another bee is dancing!
She's found a garden
full of flowers.

She waggles her bottom.
She crawls in circles.
Her dance shows Busy Bee
how to find the garden.

Busy Bee and thousands like her fly from the hive.

They find the garden
full of flowers.
They drink the nectar.
They take the pollen.
Busy Bee has work to do.

Picture Word List

hive
page 5

drone
page 16

nectar
page 9

queen
bee
page 17

pollen
page 10

bee grub
page 18

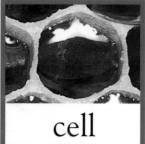

cell
page 14

feelers
page 24